DIGITAL MARKETING HANDBOOK

FOR ESTATE PLANNING ATTORNEYS

COOPER SAUNDERS

Copyright © 2024 by Cooper Saunders

All rights reserved.

No part of this book may be reproduced in any form or by any electronic or mechanical means, including information storage and retrieval systems, without written permission from the author, except for the use of brief quotations in a book review.

CONTENTS

Foreword	xi
Free Digital Marketing Course on Growing Your Estate Planning Law Firm	xxi
1. Digital Marketing Strategy	1
2. Online Basics and Tracking	11
3. Local SEO – Getting Your Firm to the Top of Local Search	37
4. Google Pay-Per-Click Ads	59
5. Generating Business With Webinars	75
6. How to Generate Referrals From Your Target Market	91
7. Putting It All Together	101
Wrapping It Up	113

WHAT CLIENTS HAVE TO SAY ABOUT WISEGUYS

"For the past eight months, I have used WiseGuys Digital Marketing to build up my online presence for my law firm, DeGioia Law, PLLC. As a solo practitioner, I don't have the time to learn about the ins and outs of SEO and Google Adwords, so I knew I needed a trustworthy marketing team from the get-go.

Many marketing companies provide low quality service for exorbitant costs. However, working with Cooper and his team has been as close to white-glove service as you can get. In the past eight months, the number of quality calls has been going up, and with WiseGuys, I feel that the sky is the limit! I wholeheartedly recommend them for any law firm that wants to take its digital marketing to the next level."

– MATTHEW DEGIOIA

"I was blessed to find WiseGuys Digital Marketing. Prior to finding this marketing firm, I had used countless others. I believe I was using 3 to 4 marketing firms at the time I contacted WiseGuys. I contacted WiseGuys because an attorney on LinkedIn recommended them. It was a year or two before I decided to reach out to them because I was nervous about the expense and skeptical about marketing agencies. I asked if they would be willing to work on just my GMB profile before I agreed to move forward with them with additional services.

The Team led by Cooper Saunders made a relatively fast impact on my GMB profile. I noticed my leads increasing and was eager to find out what else they could do. The expense of moving from GMB to their full services was large for me at the time, but I went for it. I let Cooper know that I wanted to hire an associate attorney and pay her at least $80K to $90K per year within two to three months of working with each other.

Because of WiseGuys' efforts, I was able to make this plan a reality. WiseGuys is a marketing firm I plan to stay with for years to come. Cooper is down to earth, friendly, and works to meet me and my law firm where we are at any given time. At this point, I consider Cooper a friend and feel blessed to have him in my life."

– JAIME V. PAPA, ESQ.

"After hiring countless Gurus and growing tired of lighting tens of thousands of dollars on fire, I was introduced to WiseGuys Digital Marketing by a fellow estate planning attorney. We made the leap after being shown (with actual data) that our current SEO campaign wasn't cutting it.

My only regret is not finding these guys sooner! A few months in and we're already up 40% during our SLOW season! I'm excited about the opportunities this growth will provide us and look forward to working with this crew for all of our SEO, Google Ads, and digital advertising needs."

– MICHAEL JENKINS

"Cooper and his WiseGuys Team are out of this world. I've managed my own SEO, Website Development, and Google Ads for over 6 years, and I have met dozens of digital marketing agencies…NO ONE has even come close to as knowledgeable as Cooper. Couple that with his hard work and dedication to doing things the right way, and you have a winning strategy.

Cooper is hands-down the best in the industry. I only have one regret—that I didn't meet him 6 years ago!"

– ANDREW ZIHMER

"I opened my law practice in August 2023. I started from zero visibility for my firm. I hired Cooper from day one to take care of my Local SEO, and he has crushed it! Within 6 months, I went from way, way, way, way, way down the search page to within the top 3 in organic searches. I don't know what he does, but it works! I highly recommend Cooper and his team. His team also developed my website. People are constantly telling me how great it looks—so great job on that as well!"

– TANYA HENDRIX

"I have been in practice and business long enough to know that it's nearly impossible to guarantee anything. Too many times I had heard of marketing companies promising one thing and not being able to quite deliver on those lofty expectations immediately.

Fortunately, I was introduced to Cooper Saunders, owner of WiseGuys Digital Marketing. Cooper was transparent about what success looks like in both the short term and long term, brainstorms with me regularly with actual data in my market about how to tweak my messaging, and I definitely view him as more of a trusted advisor beyond the scope of marketing services.

He built my website, and we are now working together on my Google Ads. We tried a few different strategies and recently started a new campaign about 3 weeks ago. I have started receiving calls from prospects nearly every day. And one of those from this week signed on as a pretty substantial client just this morning."

– DAVE STROUSBERG

FOREWORD

December 27, 2017. As most families across the country took an evening to slow down and reflect on Christmas, I sat on the sofa with my laptop open, wrapping up the QuickBooks for the end of the year. Tracy had launched Zihmer Law Firm just nine months earlier. While she was a very accomplished estates and trusts attorney, neither of us had run a business before. Every day was hard. I was just thankful to have a few days off from my job as an engineer so that I could focus on the law firm.

Tracy sat down next to me on the sofa and flipped my world upside down. "I know we talked about you coming into the law firm full time in four or five years. I don't want to wait that long. You should quit your job now."

FOREWORD

I sat there in shock and disbelief. This wasn't the plan, and it wasn't what we had been talking about. The law firm wasn't even close to replacing both of our salaries. Tracy could sense my objection. What she said next will live with me for the rest of my days.

"I believe in you, and I believe in us."

I joined Tracy at the law firm three months later. The next six years took me on a journey where I learned as much about running a law firm as I learned about myself. I fought tooth and nail to ensure that our law firm didn't just survive—I put my heart and soul into making it thrive. Together with Tracy, we made Zihmer Law Firm a million-dollar law firm in 2022. During these years, I discovered the principles of what turns law firms into high-functioning businesses. These have become what I call the Vertex Pillars.

My name is Andrew Zihmer.

I'm a husband.

I'm a father.

I'm an entrepreneur.

And most importantly...

FOREWORD

I know what it's like to burn your ship, have no backup plan, and succeed.

Today, I guide law firm owners to build the law firm (and business) of their dreams. Do

these lawyers that I work with make more money? Yes. I want everyone to go on lots of vacations, have fun, take random days off, and make memories. At the end of the day, I help attorneys build a law firm that achieves financial success without burning the candle at both ends. Tracy and I are proof that you can love your career, own a successful business, and be home for dinner.

Years ago, I didn't set out to be an expert in marketing, branding, sales, and intake for estate planning law firms. It was never my goal to find ways to automate, streamline, and build systems and processes for law firm owners to do efficient legal work.

Life has a funny way of finding us. As Tony Robbins says, "Life happens for you, not to you." Never in a million years did I think I would become a Google Ads expert. Before I met Tracy, I didn't even know what estate planning was. I'm proof that life happens for you (if you allow it).

I've spent over 2,600 hours learning how to dominate Google Ads. I have studied, learned, and implemented every lesson that I could get my hands on. As of 2024, the total revenue related to Google Ads at our estate planning law firm is over $4,000,000.

Word began to spread about my success with Google Ads and SEO. I would hop on a Zoom call with anyone who wanted to pick my brain. I was happy to share the lessons that I had learned. Word began spreading faster. I was getting interview requests for podcasts and shows. I traveled to speak with people about how Google Ads and SEO could change their law firm – but more importantly, that it could change their lives.

On January 1, 2023, I launched a new business with Tracy—Vertex League. It was the first coaching and mastermind group for estate planning law firm owners exclusively around business principles. This wasn't to teach estate planning or how to practice law.

Vertex League exists to help law firm owners grow and scale their law firms while getting out of the day-to-day operations of a law firm. Our collective guiding principles are the Vertex Pillars: marketing, systems, and leadership.

Shortly after creating Vertex League, I met with Miller Leonard, an attorney out of Colorado who had an estate planning practice. When Miller learned about Vertex League, his eyes lit up. He told me that lawyers needed help on the business front because it wasn't taught in law school.

Miller and I were on a Zoom call, and he was telling me how he had a fantastic digital marketing company doing work for him. The whole call was Miller telling me about their great work, and more importantly – the results. Before I could ask, Miller started telling me about case studies and showing me reports. Finally, I had to ask him, "Who are you working with?"

Without skipping a beat, Miller spoke up. "I'm working with Cooper Saunders. Do you want me to connect the two of you?" I quickly said yes.

Cooper and I scheduled a Zoom call for a chilly Friday in February. I felt like I was bursting at the seams. "I've been running Google Ads and doing SEO with a lot of success. What kinds of campaigns do you run?"

He rattled off the campaign types and bid strategies that he was using for estate planning clients. I asked Cooper point blank, "Why do you set them up that way?"

Cooper offered to share his screen and gave me a glimpse into how he did his work. My eyes went wide open. It was incredibly similar to what we were doing at Zihmer Law Firm! For every data point I asked about, Cooper gave me a real answer. Cost per lead. Cost per click. Budget spend. Strategy. Conversion tracking.

I realized that Cooper was doing things how I did them. More importantly, I knew just how well these strategies worked. We spent over an hour getting into the nitty gritty details of how the search algorithms work. The two of us were sharing ideas and having our own mastermind session on Google Ads. I know a lot of people in the marketing space, and this was the first person that I ever met who knew more about Google Ads than me.

About six months later, an estate planning law firm owner in my mastermind group reached out to me. "Hey, I've implemented your lessons on Google Ads, and we are making money. It works. But I have a problem." Oh no. My heart sank.

He continued, "The problem is that running Google Ads myself is taking up a lot of my time. Now, I can't do the actual legal work. Is there any chance that you have someone that could take over my Google Ads that does it like you do?"

"Yes! I've been under the hood of how this guy does this, and I can tell you he's legit."

I connected this attorney with Cooper, and off they went. If you've seen case studies of Cooper's work, then you have read this law firm's story. I won't give away the personal details here, but I can vouch that it is 100% true and accurate. The law firm owner took my lessons and implemented them. But as people learn, it is a ton of work. This attorney wanted to hire a Google Ads expert who does it the right way so that the law firm owner could focus on the things he's amazing at.

This is just one of many examples that I could give you of my inner circle working with Cooper. He has made MILLIONS of dollars for the lawyers in Vertex League.

Google Ads works. It works because Google is the most trusted and most used search engine on the planet. There are over 6.3 million searches every minute, every single day, day after day. If you aren't taking advantage of that user base, then you are missing out. For the law firm owners out there, especially estate planning, this works.

The revenue that we've generated from Google Ads and SEO allows me to take 70+ days off every year, take the kids to Disney 2-3 times per year, fly first class, buy fun cars, take random days off to play at the park, and simply enjoy life. Our firm is on pace for nearly $2M this year and revenue from Google is a very substantial part of that. If you aren't using Google Ads and Google SEO in your law firm, then I have to ask: what are you waiting for?

I don't share these details to impress you. For some of you reading this, that is a ton of money and revenue. For others, it's nothing. I share it to demonstrate what is possible when you learn, implement, and leverage the knowledge and wisdom of a master Google Ads and SEO marketer like Cooper Saunders.

This book is your ticket to success.

The man that you are about to study and learn from is truly an amazing person. He's a smart, talented, and hardworking man. He has integrity. He is full of character. I'm proud to call him my friend.

My hope for you is that you take the lessons of this book to heart. Take time to study them and reflect on them. Understand how to implement them inside of your law firm. Because if you do this, I promise that you are giving yourself a chance to succeed at the highest levels, just like I have.

FOREWORD

Get your favorite highlighter, a pen, and your notebook by your side. Fill up your glass of water and get into your comfortable seat. You are about to embark on a journey that will not just change your law firm but that will change your life.

Study. Implement. Reap the rewards.

Andrew Zihmer
Founder, Vertex League
Vice President, Zihmer Law Firm

FREE DIGITAL MARKETING COURSE ON GROWING YOUR ESTATE PLANNING LAW FIRM

Make sure you take advantage of the completely free digital marketing course that accompanies this book. In this course, I break down in detail the exact steps you need to take to transform your estate planning law firm into a growth machine.

For the free course, visit:

estatelawyerdigitalmarketing.com

CHAPTER 1
DIGITAL MARKETING STRATEGY

If you've picked up this book, it is for one reason and one reason only: to grow your estate planning law firm. But the path to sustainable growth has never been more challenging for estate planning attorneys. Evolving client expectations, intensifying competition, and the complexities of modern digital marketing have raised the stakes considerably.

Prospective clients now tend to have very different criteria for hiring an estate planning firm versus even just 5-10 years ago. They crave convenience, demand transparency, expect seamless technology integration, and, above all, prioritize firms that can guide them through the process with empathy and emotional intelligence. Simply having legal expertise is no longer enough to attract ideal clientele consistently.

At the same time, you're likely facing intense competition not just from other local firms but also from non-traditional national brands and online-only services that are well-funded marketing machines that are making it harder than ever for smaller practices to get noticed in their own backyards.

And when you do manage to capture a prospect's attention, you then have to run the gauntlet of nurturing them into a paying client. An unintuitive website, lack of online reviews, or other misaligned marketing touchpoints along the way can disrupt the entire conversion funnel.

So, what is the common thread undermining estate planning growth? Many firms simply aren't keeping up with how consumers are making buying decisions.

HOW YOUR CONSUMERS BUY

So, how do your clients make buying decisions? There is a core group of marketing activities that produce the greatest return for estate planning lawyers. This is the Pareto Principle for marketing your estate planning law firm. The Pareto Principle states that 80 percent of the results you achieve are from 20 percent of your actions. In this book, we will dive into the 20 percent of marketing activities you need to get right before moving on to anything else. After you get these core marketing activities down, then you can experiment with other avenues, but for now, stick with the methods that are proven to generate results.

Effective marketing for estate planning firms boils down to focusing on the right things and ignoring everything else. For example, a 100-watt light bulb and a 100-watt laser both produce the same amount of energy, but their effects differ dramatically. While the light bulb can illuminate a room, the laser can cut through steel.

The core marketing activities you need to utilize before anything else are:

- Online Basics
- Website
- Local SEO
- Google Ads
- Social Media Ads
- Dream 100 Strategy

Each chapter will break down these exact steps so that you can implement them for your own practice. Now, if you are like most of my clients, you simply don't have the time to manually implement these strategies for your own law firm. If that is the case, reach out to me at Cooper@wiseguysdigitalmarketing.com, and I can break down our processes and how we can implement them for your law firm.

WATCH OUT FOR THE "GURUS"

Nine times out of ten, when I meet with a potential client for the first time, I hear a rendition of this line: "I hired a digital marketing company in the past, and they didn't generate any results. It was an awful experience."

How do you ensure you don't fall victim to the same thing again or for the first time? Ask for case studies and previous results from the digital marketing company you are thinking about hiring. If not, these "digital marketing gurus" will promise the world but will generate poor results.

When I work with an estate planning client, I put myself in their shoes—I take their firm's success as seriously as if it were my own business. Too many marketing "experts" make lofty promises without ever implementing their own recommendations or delivering actual results.

Over the past eight years, I've helped over 100 estate planning firms across the country expand their books of business using digital marketing tactics that really move the needle. Don't let your law firm be a digital marketing agency's guinea pig!

DISCLAIMER

But before we get into marketing techniques, I need to get something off my chest. I am not a silver bullet. No marketer is, no matter what they say in their pitch. I can only do so much if you don't have the right foundation in place. I can get a lead to raise their hand and contact your firm.

After the lead expresses interest, there are a few things you need to take ownership of.

- Making the sale
- Setting up an outstanding intake process
- Do a good job and generate outstanding word-of-mouth

The truth is, any marketer ethical enough to want your long-term success will be upfront that there are no shortcuts or silver bullets. Effective marketing is simply the combined result of steadfast commitment to proven strategies, diligent execution of best practices, and continual optimization through a data-driven approach tailored to your specific business goals and audience.

I'm no exception. As skilled as my team may be, I can only be as effective as the commitment and foundational systems you have in place at your firm. My role is to strategically drive leads into your pipeline through proven digital marketing strategies and techniques. But from there, your firm's ability to provide outstanding client experiences, generate positive word-of-mouth, implement retention processes, and deliver top-notch legal work is equally critical.

With that caveat out of the way, let's look at a recent case study highlighting how WiseGuys Digital Marketing helped transform an estate planning practice into a seven-figure business.

THE CASE STUDY

Jenkins and Jenkins Estate Planning Lawyers reached out to WiseGuys Digital Marketing with a specific goal in mind: to elevate their law firm into a seven-figure business. During our initial consultation, I saw the look I see time and time again when meeting estate planning lawyers.

You could tell he was sick of getting the run around from digital marketing agencies and just wanted someone he could trust to get the job done. Michael and I met during a presentation I gave to a group of estate planning lawyers called Vertex League, which Andrew Zihmer runs. If you don't know who Andrew Zihmer is, you need to get in touch with him.

Michael told me he had used a couple of digital marketing companies in the past, and they were very inconsistent. He wanted to see how I would be different.

I asked him what the other digital marketing companies had done for him in the past. He explained that they handled his local SEO and Google Ads.

My approach is different from that of most digital marketing companies. Instead of telling him what my company offered and giving him a blanket pitch, I asked if I could share my screen and show him some stuff. I am big on education-based selling.

When my screen appeared, I walked him through the issues his local SEO campaign was having and why his rankings had stagnated for so long. I opened another estate planning client we had in Chicago, and we were ranking number one for around sixty keywords. I showed him the plan we implemented for them and what results it would generate for his law firm.

Then, I opened the Google Keyword Planner to show him how many leads we could generate through Google ads and approximately how much he would have to invest per lead.

He was amazed. He told me that out of all the meetings with digital marketers he has worked with, they have never shown him what they can do with actual proof and data to back it up.

And the rest is history.

> "If January is any indication of how this year will go, it should be absolute insanity. YTD for '24 compared to this time in '23, we're up 420% in collected revenue... doesn't even seem real to see that kind of metric."
>
> – MICHAEL JENKINS

For Michael Jenkins' video testimonial, visit:

EstateLawyerDigitalMarketing.com/jj.

Are you ready to take your estate planning practice to the next level? Let's get started.

CHAPTER 2
ONLINE BASICS AND TRACKING

Before diving into more advanced marketing strategies for your estate planning law firm, it's essential to establish a solid online foundation. These basic building blocks will support all your future marketing efforts and help ensure your success. Think of these elements as the cornerstone of your digital marketing strategy. The key building blocks to focus on are:

- Target Market
- Branding
- Website
- Expert Status
- Social Proof
- Social Media
- Tracking

IT'S NOT EVERYONE

Before you can effectively brand your estate planning law firm or market your services, defining your target market is crucial. Your target market is the specific group of people who are most likely to need and benefit from your services. By understanding who these individuals are, you can tailor your marketing efforts to resonate with them directly, ensuring that your messages are both relevant and compelling.

WHY DEFINING YOUR TARGET MARKET MATTERS

1. **Focused Marketing Efforts:** Knowing your target market allows you to focus your marketing efforts on the people most likely to become clients. This focused approach saves time, money, and resources by eliminating broad, generalized marketing strategies that may not yield results. Instead, you can craft personalized messages that speak directly to the needs and concerns of your ideal clients.
2. **Tailored Branding:** When you understand your target market, you can create a brand identity that resonates with them. From your

firm's name to the colors you use and the tone of your messaging, every aspect of your brand should reflect the values and preferences of your target audience. A brand that aligns with the needs of your ideal clients will make a stronger impression and foster a sense of connection and trust.

3. **Improved Client Relationships:** By identifying your target market, you can better understand their needs, pain points, and preferences. This insight lets you provide more personalized and relevant services, enhancing client satisfaction and building long-term relationships. When clients feel understood and valued, they are more likely to refer your services to others, driving word-of-mouth growth.

4. **Efficient Use of Resources:** Marketing budgets are not unlimited, so it's important to use your resources wisely. Targeting a specific market ensures that your advertising dollars are spent reaching people who are more likely to need your services, maximizing your return on investment. Whether through digital ads, social media campaigns, or direct mail, knowing your audience lets you make strategic decisions

about where to allocate your marketing budget.

5. **Competitive Advantage:** A well-defined target market helps you stand out from competitors, taking a more generic approach. You establish a niche that makes you more memorable and desirable by positioning your firm as the go-to expert for a specific group, such as high-net-worth individuals, young families, or business owners. Specializing in a target market can also allow you to command higher fees as you are seen as the expert in that particular field.

HOW TO DEFINE YOUR TARGET MARKET

1. **Analyze Your Current Clients:** Start by looking at your existing client base. Who are your best clients? What do they have in common in terms of demographics, interests, or needs? Identifying patterns among your current clients can provide valuable insights into the types of people who are most likely to benefit from your services.
2. **Consider Market Segments:** Think about the different segments within the estate

planning market that you might serve. For example, your target market could include retirees planning for their legacy, young families looking to secure their children's future, business owners concerned about succession planning, or high-net-worth individuals seeking complex estate strategies. Each segment has unique needs and concerns, so deciding which segment best aligns with your expertise and goals is important.

3. **Research Competitors:** Look at what other estate planning law firms in your area are doing. Who are they targeting, and what services are they offering? This research can help you identify gaps in the market and opportunities to differentiate your firm by focusing on underserved or niche areas.

4. **Identify Pain Points:** Understand your potential clients' specific challenges and concerns. What are the common issues that drive people to seek estate planning services? Whether it's protecting assets from taxes, ensuring the care of minor children, or avoiding probate, knowing these pain points will allow you to address them directly in your marketing and service offerings.

5. **Create Client Personas:** Develop detailed profiles of your ideal clients, known as client personas. These personas should include demographic information (age, income, marital status) as well as psychographic details (values, goals, fears). By putting a "face" to your target market, you can better tailor your messaging and services to meet their needs.

ADAPTING YOUR STRATEGY OVER TIME

Choosing a target market is not a one-time task. It's important to regularly review and refine your target market as your business grows and evolves. Market conditions, client needs, and your firm's services may change, and your target market may need to be adjusted accordingly. Stay informed about industry trends, listen to client feedback, and continuously analyze your market to ensure your marketing strategies remain effective.

MOVING FORWARD WITH A CLEAR FOCUS

Defining your target market is the foundation of successful branding and marketing. Once you clearly understand who your ideal clients are, you can create a brand identity that resonates with them, craft marketing messages that capture their attention, and offer services that meet their specific needs. When looking at your competitors, I can almost guarantee you that 99% of them lack focus.

By focusing on the right audience, you can set your estate planning law firm up for long-term success, build a strong client base, and establish your firm as a trusted authority.

BRANDING

When done correctly, your brand does two critical jobs: it makes your firm synonymous with your services in the minds of your target market and enhances your visibility on search engines. Your brand is more than just your firm's name; it encompasses your visual identity, messaging, and the overall perception people have of your law firm.

I recall a meeting with a lawyer who was setting up his estate planning practice. He wanted to name his firm "Monarch Law." While this name sounded elegant, it didn't convey what services the firm offered. If potential clients and search engines can't immediately tell what you do, they might overlook your firm. I recommended a name like "The Monarch Estate Planning Law Firm," which instantly communicates the firm's specialty. This makes it easier for clients to understand your services and improves your search engine ranking by incorporating relevant keywords.

The lawyer questioned, "But what about big brands like Nike or law firms that use vague names? They seem to do just fine." True, big brands have established their names over decades, often with massive marketing budgets. For a smaller or new firm (or people who don't enjoy lighting money on fire), it's wiser to choose a name that directly reflects your services, making it easier for potential clients to find and trust you without a huge marketing investment.

THE PSYCHOLOGY OF COLOR

Color is a powerful tool in branding, affecting perception and influencing emotions. The colors you choose for your law firm's branding can convey subconscious messages and significantly impact client decisions. Here's how different colors might affect your brand:

- **Green:** Often associated with nature, growth, and stability. A deep green can symbolize wealth, security, and reliability for estate planning firms, reassuring clients that their assets and legacy are in good hands. Lighter greens can evoke health and balance, appealing to clients who prioritize holistic and careful planning for their future.

- **Red:** While red is a strong, attention-grabbing color, it needs to be used carefully. Bright red can evoke passion and urgency, making it suitable for calls to action, while darker shades like burgundy can convey luxury and exclusivity. Overusing red, however, can suggest danger or alarm, which is not ideal for estate planning.
- **Blue:** Universally linked to trust, professionalism, and calm. Light blue can give a sense of openness and approachability, while darker blues like navy convey authority and seriousness. Blue is a safe and effective color for law firms looking to instill confidence and reliability in their clients.
- **Neutrals:** Colors like black, gray, and white are timeless and convey sophistication, simplicity, and professionalism. A combination of these colors can create a high-end, classic feel that is appealing to clients with significant assets who expect a premium

service. Be cautious not to overuse cool grays, which can appear cold or uninviting.
- **Purple/Violet:** These colors can add a unique touch of creativity and luxury. Lighter purples can evoke a sense of nostalgia and sentimentality, while deeper purples, like plum, suggest wealth and ambition. These colors work well for firms looking to distinguish themselves from more traditional competitors and appeal to clients seeking innovative solutions.

To ensure consistency, document your brand colors with the specific color codes. Consistent use of colors across all platforms helps build brand recognition and reinforces your firm's image whenever clients interact with your marketing materials.

LOGO AND GRAPHICS

Your logo is often the first visual representation of your brand that potential clients will see. A professional, well-designed logo that incorporates your brand colors and aligns with your firm's identity is crucial. Avoid creating your logo using generic templates or low-quality design tools. Instead, invest in a skilled graphic designer who can develop a unique, memorable logo and branding guide that conveys your firm's core values. This doesn't have to be expensive; you can get a great logo anywhere between $50 to $200.

Ensure you receive the logo in multiple formats (JPEG, PNG, SVG) and sizes to use across different platforms, from your website to social media profiles and printed materials. The right logo not only helps with brand recognition but also establishes a sense of trust and professionalism.

PERSONALIZATION

Adding a personal touch to your branding is vital in today's market. Consumers want to connect with real people, not faceless entities. Personalization helps create an emotional bond between your firm and potential clients, fostering trust and loyalty.

One effective way to personalize your branding is through professional photography and video content. High-quality images of your attorneys at work, engaging with clients, or participating in community events can humanize your brand. Video content allows you to go even further by showcasing your legal team's personalities, expertise, and passions. For example:

- **Attorney Introduction Videos:** Short clips where each attorney introduces themselves, shares their background and explains why they are passionate about estate planning. This builds rapport and trust before the client even meets them.
- **Office Tours and Team Videos:** Give potential clients a behind-the-scenes look at your office environment, showcasing a welcoming and professional atmosphere. Highlight team interactions to convey a sense of collaboration and warmth.
- **Service Explanation Videos:** Short videos that explain complex estate planning topics in simple terms can help educate potential clients and position your firm as knowledgeable and approachable.
- **Process Walkthrough Videos:** Show potential clients what to expect when they engage your firm. A step-by-step guide through the estate planning process can demystify the experience and alleviate fears of the unknown.
- **Client Testimonial Videos:** Highlight satisfied clients sharing their positive experiences. Testimonials are powerful tools for building trust and credibility.

Beyond visual content, personalize your written communications. Share your firm's story, the challenges you've overcome, and your commitment to your clients. Include attorney biographies that provide personal anecdotes and insights into their professional motivations. The more clients know about you as individuals, the more likely they are to feel connected and trust your firm.

WEBSITE BASICS

Your website is the digital hub of your law firm and plays a critical role in converting visitors into leads. A well-designed website should be visually appealing, easy to navigate, and optimized for conversions. Here are some key elements to focus on:

MOBILE-FIRST DESIGN

With over half of web traffic coming from mobile devices, your website must be designed with a mobile-first approach. This means that every element, from navigation to content layout, should be optimized for smartphones and tablets. Mobile users expect fast-loading pages, readable text, and buttons that are easy to tap. Avoid designs requiring users to pinch, zoom, or scroll excessively to find information.

A seamless mobile experience ensures that potential clients can easily engage with your content and contact your firm, regardless of the device they use.

INTUITIVE NAVIGATION AND USER EXPERIENCE (UX)

Your website's navigation should be straightforward and intuitive. Avoid cluttered menus or unnecessary pages that confuse visitors. The most important information—such as your practice areas, attorney profiles, and contact information—should be easily accessible. Use clear calls-to-action (CTAs) like "Schedule a Consultation" or "Call Us Today" prominently throughout your site.

Consider using "sticky" navigation bars that remain visible as users scroll, making it easy for them to access other sections of your site. Place contact forms in strategic locations, such as the homepage, service pages, and the footer, to encourage inquiries. A well-thought-out UX improves the visitor experience and increases the likelihood of converting them into clients.

COMPELLING COPY AND MESSAGING

Your website's content should clearly articulate your value propositions and differentiate your firm from competitors. Avoid legal jargon and overly complex language. Instead, write in a conversational tone that speaks directly to your client's needs and concerns. Use storytelling techniques to connect with readers on an emotional level.

Implement the "Problem-Agitate-Solve" framework in your content:

1. **Problem:** Identify common challenges clients face in estate planning, such as protecting assets or ensuring their wishes are honored.
2. **Agitate:** Highlight the potential risks or consequences of not addressing these issues, creating a sense of urgency.
3. **Solve:** Present your firm's unique solutions, emphasizing how your expertise and personalized approach can provide peace of mind and effective estate planning.

Incorporate client success stories, case studies, and examples that illustrate how your firm has successfully helped clients in the past. This not only builds credibility but also helps prospective clients see the value you bring.

SOCIAL PROOF

Trust is a critical factor in choosing a law firm, and social proof is one of the most effective ways to build it. Social proof includes:

- **Client Testimonials:** Written or video testimonials from satisfied clients that describe their positive experiences with your firm.
- **Google Reviews:** Display your Google Reviews prominently on your website. Encourage satisfied clients to leave reviews, which will not only boost your credibility but also improve your local SEO.
- **Accreditations and Awards:** Showcase any industry certifications, memberships, or awards your firm has received. These act as third-party endorsements that enhance your firm's credibility.
- **Media Mentions:** If your firm has been featured in news articles, podcasts, or other media, highlight these mentions to showcase your expertise and recognition.

Integrating social proof throughout your website reassures potential clients that your firm is trusted and respected in the community, making them more likely to reach out.

YOUR ABOUT US PAGE

The About Us page is often one of the most visited pages on a law firm's website. This is your opportunity to connect with potential clients on a personal level. Here's how to structure it effectively:

1. **Your Story:** Share the origin story of your firm. Explain why you chose to focus on estate planning and what drives your team to provide exceptional service. Highlight your mission and core values, making it clear what sets your firm apart.
2. **The Characters:** Introduce the people behind your firm. Include professional headshots and detailed bios for each attorney, emphasizing their experience, areas of expertise, and personal interests. Links to LinkedIn profiles can add further credibility.
3. **The Conflict:** Describe the challenges or gaps in the legal market that motivated you to start your firm. This could be a personal

experience or an industry-wide issue that you wanted to address.
4. **The Resolution:** Explain how your firm addresses these challenges. Highlight your firm's successes, client testimonials, and awards that demonstrate your ability to deliver positive outcomes.
5. **The Dialogue:** Define your firm's tone and voice. How do you communicate with clients? This section should include a video introduction or "About Us" video that encapsulates your firm's personality and approach.
6. **The Call to Action:** Make it easy for potential clients to take the next step. Provide a clear and singular call to action, such as scheduling a consultation or calling your firm.
7. **The Setting:** Showcase your office environment with photos and descriptions. This helps clients visualize your firm and adds a personal touch. Include images of your office, meeting spaces, and any awards or recognitions displayed.

An engaging and well-structured About Us page helps build a connection with potential clients, encouraging them to trust your firm and take action.

EXPERT STATUS

Positioning yourself as an expert is critical in the legal field. Clients want to know they are working with someone who has deep knowledge and experience. One powerful way to establish expert status is by creating authoritative content that demonstrates your expertise. Things such as blogs, eBooks, podcasts, and guides will establish your credibility and allow your target market to see you as the expert in your field. But, there is one tool that is my favorite that will allow you to be seen as the expert in your field, and that is publishing a book.

WRITING A BOOK

Another tool that has really helped my clients to be seen as experts is to write "the book" on the subject of estate planning. Again, being seen as the expert in your niche is critical as a lawyer. Your potential clients want to know the law firm they hire knows what they are doing and is the expert in their field. Another perk is that you can charge more than your competitors when you are seen as the expert.

One of the greatest ways to do this is to "write the book" on the subject. Nothing is more powerful than meeting with a potential client and pulling out a book you wrote that covers the subject they are considering hiring you for.

There are a handful of benefits when you have a published book.

- No one throws away books. You will remain on their bookshelf for life.
- You will gain immediate trust with your potential client
- You can offer it as a lead magnet
- You will be seen as the expert

To ensure you get the most out of your hard work in writing this content, you need to do the following. Once you have the content all written out, you need to get a cover created and the interior formatted by a professional. Again, email me at Cooper@wiseguysdm.com if you need help with this. My team has done a handful in the past year alone. The total of pages your book needs to be is around 50-60 pages at minimum. This way, you can upload it to Amazon KDP, which will allow you to have a book that is published and printed on demand and will allow you to create an author page.

If you Google my name, Cooper Saunders, you will see I have a Google Knowledge Panel. This is massive in terms of my reputation and visibility. When someone Googles you, and you have a knowledge panel like the celebrities do, making sales and growing your law firm will be a breeze!

Now, are you going to sell more books than the Harry Potter series? No way. But if you are anything like me, the revenue it will generate for your law firm will be immense.

HOSTING WEBINARS

Webinars are an interactive and engaging way to share your knowledge, connect with potential clients, and establish your firm as the go-to resource for estate planning. In a later chapter, I will cover how you can use webinars to generate new business, but for now, here is how you can use webinars to establish yourself as an expert.

- **Interactivity:** Live webinars allow you to interact directly with attendees, answer questions in real time, and address specific concerns. This builds trust and showcases your expertise.

- **Lead Generation:** Webinars require registration, which helps you collect contact information from interested prospects. Follow up with attendees after the webinar to nurture leads and move them closer to becoming clients.
- **Exclusivity:** The format of live webinars creates a sense of exclusivity and value. Clients feel they are receiving special insights directly from an expert.
- **Repurposing Content:** Record your webinars and use the content in multiple ways. Post the recordings on your website and YouTube, share clips on social media, and use the audio for podcasts. Transcribe the webinars into blog posts to expand your reach and enhance your SEO.

A well-executed webinar strategy can position your firm as an authority in estate planning, generate high-quality leads, and provide valuable content for ongoing marketing efforts.

SOCIAL MEDIA

Social media is an essential platform for building relationships, showcasing expertise, and generating leads. However, a thoughtful approach is required to be effective. Rather than directly pitching your services, focus on creating engaging and informative content that resonates with your audience. Here's how to make the most of social media:

CONTENT STRATEGY

Develop a content strategy that includes a mix of educational posts, community engagement, and testimonials. Repurpose content from your webinars, blog posts, and videos. Use social media to share:

- **Tips and Advice:** Offer practical estate planning tips and advice that potential clients will find useful. This not only provides value but also positions your firm as a knowledgeable resource.
- **Case Studies and Success Stories:** Share anonymized case studies that highlight how your firm has helped clients achieve their estate planning goals. This demonstrates your expertise and builds trust.
- **Behind-the-Scenes Content:** Show the human side of your firm by sharing behind-the-scenes photos and videos. This could

include team events, office culture, and community involvement.

ENGAGEMENT AND INTERACTION

Social media is not just a broadcast channel; it's a platform for interaction. Respond to comments, answer questions, and engage with your audience regularly. Encourage followers to share their own experiences or ask questions about estate planning. This two-way communication helps build a loyal and engaged community.

THE IMPORTANCE OF TRACKING

Tracking is vital for understanding the effectiveness of your marketing efforts. Every month when I meet with my clients, I show them which marketing avenue is producing the highest return on investment. Without being able to track and understand where the best leads are coming from for your law firm, marketing will be a nightmare.

Without proper tracking, you're operating in the dark, unable to determine what's working and what isn't. Here are the key tracking tools to consider:

- **Call Tracking:** Use call tracking software like CallRail to track phone calls generated by specific marketing campaigns. This helps you measure the ROI of your ads and identify which channels are driving leads.
- **Customer Relationship Management (CRM):** Implement a CRM system like Hubspot, Lawmatics, or Clio to manage client interactions and track lead progress. CRMs provide valuable insights into your sales pipeline and help you manage follow-ups effectively.
- **Google Analytics:** Use Google Analytics to track website traffic, user behavior, and conversion rates. Set up goals to track specific actions, such as form submissions, downloads, or webinar registrations.
- **Conversion Tracking:** Implement conversion tracking for all your online marketing efforts, including Google Ads, social media ads, and email campaigns. This allows you to measure the effectiveness of each campaign and make data-driven decisions to optimize your marketing strategy.

WRAPPING IT UP

Setting up a solid online foundation with effective branding, a high-quality website, expert status, social proof, social media presence, and tracking capabilities is essential for your estate planning firm's long-term success. These basics will not only help you attract more clients but also ensure that your marketing efforts are efficient and effective. Establishing these building blocks before moving on to more advanced techniques will save time, money, and effort, ultimately leading to a stronger, more successful marketing strategy.

Let's move on to tactics and strategies to bring more cases to your law firm.

CHAPTER 3
LOCAL SEO – GETTING YOUR FIRM TO THE TOP OF LOCAL SEARCH

When it comes to consistently bringing in new cases, ranking number one in the Local Map Pack is the key. Here's why:

Just think about how you use search yourself—when looking for a local service provider like a lawyer, plumber, or restaurant, chances are you look at the top three results and call or inquire about the business with the most five-star reviews.

Your potential clients are no different. They're typing queries like "estate planning attorney near me" into Google and likely hiring one of the first few firms that appear in those coveted Local Map Pack results.

To illustrate the immense opportunity local seo can bring to your law firm, let's look at Kansas City. Each month, around 2,500 searches for estate planning keywords occur in the metro area. Over 90% of those searches will interact with the top 3 law firms shown in the map pack listings.

Think about that for a moment. 90% out of 2,500 searches a month is 2,250 business interactions every single month.

That's an incredible amount of potential business you could be missing out on if your law firm isn't showing up in the map pack. Chances are, you're inadvertently sending all those prospective clients and revenues to your competitors who have focused on optimizing their local search presence.

The good news? By following the proper local SEO strategies, you can fight your way to the top of those map pack results and finally start capitalizing on all those valuable local leads. While SEO can seem complex, the core principles are simple once you understand them. In this chapter, I am going to walk you through the essential elements that you need to focus on to ensure your law firm ranks in the top three results for your city.

WHAT IS LOCAL SEO?

Local SEO is all about increasing your firm's visibility in search engine results for queries with local intent—i.e., people looking for estate planning services in a specific city, town, or geographic region.

Google prioritizes local businesses in these types of results thanks to the local map pack and local finder features you see at the top of the search page. The map pack displays the top three ranked businesses while clicking the local finder links expands to show more options.

So why did Google create these localized search features? A few key reasons:

- **The Rise of Mobile Internet Use**: With more people searching on smartphones, there was a need to surface locally relevant results for "near me" type queries.

- **Precision in Search Results**: Search engines strive to provide the most relevant results to users. Local SEO allows businesses to target customers in their specific area.
- **Competitive Advantage for Small Businesses:** Local SEO levels the playing field by allowing smaller businesses to compete for local queries where proximity is a factor.
- **Increased Visibility and Traffic**: Optimizing for local search helps businesses get found by more local customers and drive foot traffic.
- **Consumer Trust and Engagement**: Local listings with reviews, photos, and other business details help build trust and engagement with nearby consumers.

If you open an incognito window on Google Chrome and search "estate planning lawyer in [your city]," you'll immediately see the localized map pack and local finder results I'm referring to. Those prime listing spots at the very top of the page are absolute gold mines when it comes to driving qualified leads.

So how can you get your law firm listed in those coveted positions? It starts with understanding the key local SEO ranking factors that Google's algorithm considers.

LOCAL SEO RANKING FACTORS

Choosing Your Location

The location of your office plays an important role in determining the results you achieve from Local SEO. You see, your law firm is more than likely only going to appear in the Local Map Pack in the city you are physically located in. So if you choose a city that is way too small or way too competitive, your Local SEO efforts will be an uphill battle.

Let's look at an example real quick. Say I am looking to start a new estate planning law firm. I have already chosen a name that will allow me to automatically have an edge over my competitors since I followed the branding guidelines in chapter two. My estate planning law firm's name is "Oak Tree Estate Planning Law Firm."

When determining where I want my office to be located, I want to ensure that it is a medium to big market where my target market is located. For extra Local SEO points, include the city you want to rank for in your law firm's name. You can set up a DBA if you don't want to include it in your main law firm's name.

More than likely, you already have a city you want to dominate. If so, go after it. If you are unsure, email me at Cooper@wiseguysdm.com and I will perform a free market analysis to ensure you choose the right city that fits your goals.

Now, if you already have an office set up or want to rank in more than one city, this is 100% doable. Many of my clients have more than one office location to ensure that they can dominate more than one city in their metropolitan area.

To do this, though, you must have a legitimate physical location in the cities/areas you want to rank in. Google needs to trust that your business is actually operating and providing services in those geographic areas. More than likely, Google will have you verify your location by filming a video. Here is what they require to get your location verified.

Recording Your Business Details

- Show the surrounding area, such as street signs or neighboring businesses
- Your location should match the address you entered

- Show business name printed on permanent fixtures such as signboard
- Your business name should match the name you entered
- Access staff-only areas or unlock entrance
- You need to show you're authorized to represent this business

Service Radius Locations

If you have multiple office locations or service radius cities (like lawyers offering in-home visits or services in multiple counties), be sure to clearly define your service areas and create web pages around each of those location hubs.

Name, Address, Phone Number Citations

These refer to consistent listings of your firm's Name, Address, and Phone number across the web on directory sites, maps, apps, and more. Google cross-references these citations as a trust signal for your business's presence in a local area.

The more verified listings you have on reputable local directories (Yelp, Yellow Pages, Apple Maps, etc.) with matching NAP data, the better.

It's critical that your NAP details (business name, address formats, suite numbers, phone numbers, etc.)

are 100% consistent anywhere they are listed online—from your website to directory profiles to local chamber listings. Any inconsistencies can cancel out your local ranking abilities.

Not all citations are equal—Google prioritizes reputable, authoritative sources. You want listings from high-profile directories like Yelp, Yellow Pages, Bing, Apple Maps, and Superpages, plus industry-specific directories such as Avvo or Martindale-Hubbell.

While quality is most important, you still need a healthy overall quantity of citation listings from a diverse set of online directories, particularly locally relevant ones.

It is crucial to have your business name, address, hours, images, categories, and other details 100% complete and consistent with your other listings. Incomplete profiles will hinder your local rankings.

GOOGLE BUSINESS PROFILE

Your Google Business Profile (GBP) is the most influential local ranking factor for appearing in the Local Map Pack. You need to ensure that it signals to Google that it's optimized and relevant.

Create Or Claim Google Business Listing

To start, you need to claim or create a Google Business Listing. Without your business listing, your law firm will not rank in the Local Map Pack. The best way to check for this is to go to Google and search for your law firm. There will be text that says, "Own This Business?" Click on this and ensure it has been claimed. If it has not, go through the steps to confirm your listing.

If your law firm doesn't show up, you will need to create a brand-new listing. Open Google, and type https://www.google.com/business/. Once here, click "Manage Now," and then in the top right corner, there will be an "Add Business" button. Enter your law firm's information. They will likely have you verify by filming a video outlined above.

Business Category

Your law firm's primary category is the most important, and you must choose properly. The categories you choose will contribute to Google's determination of which searches to display your business for and determine which Google Business Profile features (like attributes, bookings, etc.) are available for you to use.

Ensure your Google Business Profile's primary business category is "Estate Planning Attorney." Surprisingly, I see "Law Firm" or "Lawyer" quite often.

Questions and Answers

Google wants Business Profiles to be a comprehensive hub for customer questions and answers related to your firm. You can preemptively answer frequently asked questions, and customers can publicly ask new questions.

Be proactive about populating and monitoring this section. It's a great way to highlight your expertise while eliminating roadblocks for prospective clients.

Services

After this, you will head over to the services tab. If you want to appear for more services than just your primary business category on Google Maps, ensure you add your additional services to your services tab in your Google Business Profile.

After you do this, write a description for each service you want to appear for. Add as many services as you can with a rich description.

Business Description

In the business description, outline the aspects of your law firm that make you unique. Throw in some of the keywords and locations you want to rank for. Such as "Estate Planning Attorney Las Vegas." Try and fill in the 750 characters with rich content about your law firm.

Photos and Videos

Visuals are a major factor that Google considers for building trust with potential customers. At a minimum, you'll want to include:

- **Logo:** Upload your logo and ensure it is the correct size. If not, email your graphic designer and ask for a 500x500 size logo.
- **Cover photo:** Use a picture of you or your team.
- **Interior photos:** Give people a glimpse inside your office and meeting areas.
- **Team photos:** Add portraits of your attorneys and key staff members.
- **Videos:** Show your firm in action through staff intros, client testimonials, etc.

The more high-quality visuals you include, the more trustworthy and credible your firm will appear in search results. Try adding 2-3 photos a week to your Google Business Profile. The more photos, the better.

Google Updates

This is Google's version of social media posting for businesses. You can publish updates, promotions, blog posts, and other timely content directly to your listing.

Aim to publish a new post weekly on estate planning news, tips, firm updates, and marketing offers. Posts allow your listing to look active and credible.

Embed Google Maps in the Footer of Your Website

Once you have created and optimized your Google Business Listing, you want to embed it into the footer of your website. This will make it easier for users to find your law firm and help Google connect the dots between your listing and your website.

WEBSITE OPTIMIZATION

My website designers and SEO team are always at war. I constantly have to remind them that a law firm's website has two main jobs. The first one, which we covered in chapter two, is to convert visitors into leads. The second one is to rank high on search engines. Both are equally important.

Here is the basic checklist you can use to get your website off to a great start.

- Develop essential pages:
- Home
- About Us
- Attorney Profiles
- Every Practice Area (Wills, Trusts, Power of Attorney, etc.)
- Contact
- FAQ
- Office location(s)
- Add a clear, unique selling proposition (USPs) and calls-to-action (CTAs).
- Ensure complete contact information is visible on the Contact page and individual location or practice area pages.
- Include a page for client testimonials and case studies.
- Links to social media, GBP profiles, and review platforms.
- Implement local business schema markup, optimize for mobile users, and ensure fast loading times.
- Secure your website with HTTPS and establish proper redirects and canonical URLs.

- Maintain consistent header tags, optimize URLs, and write unique meta descriptions and title tags for each page.

How to Write Content

When you are creating content for your website, you want to write it as if you are answering a question a potential client is asking you. For example, "What age should I get an estate plan in Missouri?"

In the first paragraph, you need to answer this question in detail. Once you have answered the question, the rest of the article needs to be supporting information on why this is the correct answer. These days, Google understands that people want the answer they are looking for as quickly as possible. When you create content in this way, it will also give your law firm a chance to rank in spot zero, which is called a featured snippet.

Location Pages

Your website should have distinct location pages for each city, neighborhood or municipality you serve. These pages should have locally relevant content, maps/embedding your specific Google Business Profile listing, staff profiles, contact information, and other signals tying your firm to those places.

Page Optimization

Individual on-page optimization factors include NAP data, keywords in the title, and domain authority. Each page of your website should follow the outline below. This will help Google understand the content on your website and what keywords you are looking to rank for.

Here's a small example of what the structure of your website page should look like:

H1: Estate Planning Law Firm In Dallas
H2: Why Choose XYZ Law
H3: Expert Estate Planning Law Firm
H3: 24 Years of Experience
H3: Over 100 Five Star Reviews
H2: How To Choose an Estate Planning Lawyer in Dallas
H3: Look at their reviews
H3: Understand their history

On-page signals are massively important for both traditional and local SEO. Your website needs to have a page for each service you offer and new content being added to it consistently.

Location-Specific Blog Content

Rather than just publishing estate planning tips and advice articles, create localized blog content that ties your insights to your service areas. For example:

- "Top 5 Estate Planning Considerations for High-Net-Worth Families in Dallas"
- "How Revocable Living Trusts Work in Naples, Florida?"

- "Trust Administration Challenges for Blended Families in Phoenix"

The titles alone signal to Google that this hyper-relevant content is centered around your local market.

Local Data/Stats Cameos

Within blog posts, webinars, guides and other content, work in references to location-specific data points and statistics that are relevant to your practice areas.

For example: "According to Maricopa County probate records, over 60% of wills filed last year had to go through some degree of litigation due to vague language or other issues." Ensure you add an outbound link to the article you found this information. Also, ensure you have it set so it opens a new window when they click the link. The last thing you want is for the visitor to leave your website and not come back.

Using localized facts and figures further cements the local theme of your content in Google's eyes.

Geo-Meta Data Optimization

Ensure all your location-specific content has optimized frontend and backend components like:

- Title tags with geo-metadata
- Header tags with city/state references
- Location-themed image alt-text
- Localized URL structures (e.g. /austin-estate-planning-guide)
- Semantic markup for geo-focused content

This helps reinforce relevance signals both for users and search engines.

Local Video Content

In addition to blogging, invest in producing video assets with a local focus as well. Ideas include:

- Localized firm overview/practice area videos
- Hyper-local webinars on location-specific laws, regulations, considerations
- Attorney vlogs or podcast series speaking directly to your local clientele
- Local client testimonial videos

Deploy these location-centric videos through YouTube, your website, and even within your Google Business Profile if they are the right-sized file. The best way to utilize these videos is to align them with the blogs you will create. This way you can really lay on the SEO butter thick!

Getting Reviews From Clients

Finally, make sure you have systematic processes in place for regularly generating new Google reviews from locally-based clients and their families. Not only are reviews a critical ranking factor, but they also add amazing hyper-local social proof.

For example, a review that says: "Michael and his team at XYZ Law Firm provided exceptional guidance in setting up our estate plan here in Portland. Their knowledge of Oregon's trust laws was invaluable..."

That ultra-local context embedded in the review itself is gold for local SEO in addition to the review rating itself.

The key premise here is to create an interwoven tapestry of location-focused content, video, data points, reviews, and other local embellishments throughout your firm's online presence.

When Google's algorithm analyzes your entire domain through that localized lens, it will have no choice but to rank you prominently for people searching in your targeted cities and geographic areas.

Don't Sleep On Bing!

Bing accounts for almost 10% of the search market, up from 6% in 2020. (https://www.impressiondigital.com/blog/bing-differ-google/) With that being said, most of the older market tend not to change their browser from Bing to Google when they buy a new computer.

There is a tool called Bing Places, which is their version of Google Business Listing. It will take around 15 minutes to create and claim your Bing Places account for your law firm; it will be well worth the time.

Keyword Research

Of course, before you can optimize for local keywords, you need to identify what phrases potential clients are actually using to search for estate planning services in your area.

If this were a typical local SEO book, I'd have you go through the tedious process of keyword research yourself. But instead, I've put together a golden asset that I'd be happy to provide you with for free. Email me at Cooper@wiseguysdm.com to get access to my complete local SEO keyword database. No need to recreate the wheel!

COMPETITOR RESEARCH

Now that you have an idea of what Google looks at when ranking local businesses, it is time to look at your competitors.

- Who ranks number one in your market?
- What does their website look like?
- How many reviews do they have?
- Have they replied to them?
- How often do they post updates on their GBP?
- What are their updates about?
- What does their cover photo look like?
- How many photos do they have?

If you email me at Cooper@wiseguysdm.com, I can run a Local Search Audit on your competitors that rank in the top three in the local map pack. This will give you an insight into what they are doing and what you can capitalize on to leapfrog them in the rankings.

WRAPPING IT UP

There is much more that goes into Local SEO, but these are the basics. An entire 300-page book could be written on the subject of Local SEO alone, but I just wanted to give you the basics that will actually help you grow in the local rankings.

But as you can see, a well-rounded local strategy that checks all the right boxes is absolutely essential for any estate planning firm looking to maximize good-fit leads from their surrounding cities and towns.

Google local search represents the biggest opportunity for consistently driving qualified cases on an ongoing basis. By systematically implementing the techniques I've outlined around optimizing your Google Business Profile, website, review acquisition, link building and more, you'll find yourself dominating those topmost local map pack results.

It takes diligent, consistent work, but the payoff is well worth it. When your law firm generates a steady influx of organic leads, you will be happy you implemented the steps in this chapter.

Let's move on to Google Ads!

CHAPTER 4
GOOGLE PAY-PER-CLICK ADS

While an optimized local SEO strategy is incredibly effective for driving sustainable lead flow over the long term, there's one inherent drawback—it takes time and consistent effort before you see full results. What if your estate planning firm needs a more immediate injection of new prospective clients into your pipeline? That's where Google Pay-Per-Click (PPC) ads come into play.

Google Ads is a powerful tool that allows you to "pay-to-play," positioning your law firm's ads at the very top of search results almost instantly for specific keywords and locations. This approach ensures that your firm's advertising appears front and center at precisely the moment someone is actively searching for estate planning services in your market. By capturing attention at the exact time prospects are looking for solutions, you can drive highly motivated leads straight into your sales funnel.

The key advantage of Google Ads is its ability to target prospects with urgent intent. Imagine the scenario: someone types "estate planning lawyer near me" into Google. With a well-crafted PPC ad, your law firm can be the first result they see, providing them with an easy and immediate way to reach out. This instant visibility turns Google Ads into a lead-generating machine. However, many law firms miss out on their full potential due to mismanagement or misunderstandings of how Google Ads works. For example, I recently consulted with a lawyer in Phoenix who was spending a hefty budget on Google Ads without seeing any return on investment. Upon reviewing his campaign, I found several optimization issues that were easily fixable. By refining his approach, I was able to turn his struggling campaign into a successful lead generator, proving that effective Google Ads can deliver substantial results.

UNDERSTANDING QUALITY SCORE: THE FOUNDATION OF SUCCESSFUL GOOGLE ADS

Before diving into the creation of a Google Ads campaign, it's essential to understand Google's Quality Score system, which directly impacts your ads' performance and cost-efficiency. Quality Score is Google's metric for evaluating the relevance and quality of your ads, keywords, and landing pages. It plays a significant role in determining your ad's placement and the cost per click. The better your Quality Score, the less you pay per click, and the higher your ad ranks. Think of Google as a massive referral engine—its goal is to provide users with the most relevant and useful results, both in organic and paid searches. A high Quality Score ensures that your ads meet these criteria.

The Four Key Components of Quality Score

1. **Click-Through Rate (CTR):** This is the percentage of people who click on your ad after seeing it. CTR is crucial because it directly indicates how appealing and relevant your ad is to users. A high CTR suggests that your ad is engaging and that the messaging resonates with the audience.

This metric tells Google that your ad is meeting the searcher's intent, thereby improving your Quality Score. To boost CTR, ensure your ad copy is compelling, includes a strong call to action, and aligns closely with the search query.

2. **Keyword/Query Relevance:** This measures how closely the keywords in your ad match the search terms used by potential clients. For example, if someone searches "Should I get a will?" and you are bidding on this query, your ad must directly address that concern. Using relevant keywords and ensuring they are included in both your ad copy and landing page content strengthens the connection between the user's search and your ad, increasing relevance and Quality Score. This alignment helps Google see your ad as a good match for the search query, improving both ad placement and effectiveness.

3. **Landing Page Quality:** This component evaluates the relevance and quality of the page users are directed to after clicking your ad. The landing page should provide valuable, original content directly related to the ad's promise. It should be easy to

navigate, load quickly, and be optimized for mobile devices. A well-designed landing page not only improves user experience but also boosts conversion rates by making it easy for visitors to take the next step, whether that's filling out a contact form or scheduling a consultation. Make sure your landing page includes clear calls to action, relevant information, and trust-building elements like client testimonials and privacy assurances.

4. **Ad Relevance:** This score reflects how closely your ad copy aligns with the keywords you're targeting. Ads that contain keywords closely related to what users are searching for tend to perform better. For example, if you're targeting the keyword "estate planning lawyer," your ad copy should directly reference estate planning services. This relevance reassures both the searcher and Google that the ad provides a solution to the searcher's query, increasing the likelihood of a click. Ad relevance is also improved by using dynamic keyword insertion, which can automatically update your ad text with the searcher's actual keywords, making your ad feel more personalized and directly relevant.

STEPS TO CREATE A HIGH-PERFORMING GOOGLE ADS PPC CAMPAIGN

To set up an effective Google Ads campaign for your estate planning firm, follow these steps:

Step 1: Create a Google Ads Account

If you don't already have one, setting up a Google Ads account is free and straightforward. Simply search "Google Ads" and follow the instructions to get started. Make sure to link your Google Ads account to your website and any relevant analytics tools to track performance accurately.

Step 2: Start a New Campaign

Once in your account, click on the "New Campaign" button. This will lead you through the setup process. Choose a campaign name that clearly identifies the purpose or target of the campaign, such as "Estate Planning Leads – August 2024." Clear naming conventions help keep your campaigns organized, especially as you scale.

Step 3: Choose Your Campaign Objective

Select "Leads" as your campaign objective. This choice will optimize your ads to encourage actions like phone calls or form submissions, which are effective for estate planning law firms. Google provides a selection of pre-set goals tailored to lead generation, making it easier to set up and track conversions.

Step 4: Select the Campaign Type

Choose "Search" campaigns, which display ads directly in Google search results when users enter relevant queries. This type of campaign is most effective for capturing immediate interest from people actively seeking legal services. You can also experiment with "Display" campaigns for broader brand awareness, but "Search" should be your primary focus for direct lead generation.

Step 5: Define Your Goals

Determine how you want to capture leads. For estate planning, generating phone calls and form submissions is often the most effective. Configure your campaign to track these actions. Use Google's built-in call-tracking features or integrate with third-party tools to ensure you're capturing all relevant lead data.

Step 6: Set Your Bidding Strategy

Opt for "Cost Per Conversion" to control how much you're willing to spend per lead. Monitor the cost per click and cost per conversion regularly to ensure a good return on investment. Use automated bidding strategies, like "Maximize Conversions," to allow Google to optimize bids in real time based on conversion likelihood.

Step 7: Target Specific Locations

Choose geographic areas where you want your ads to appear. This could be a specific city, region, or even a certain radius around your office location. Use location targeting to focus on areas where your ideal clients are most likely to be found. Exclude areas where you do not practice or where lead quality may be lower to maximize your ad spend efficiency.

Step 8: Schedule Your Ads

Use the "Ad Schedule" feature to ensure your ads run when someone is available to answer calls or respond to inquiries. This prevents wasting your budget on calls during non-business hours. For example, set your ads to run Monday through Friday, 9 AM to 5 PM, if these are your office hours. If you have staff available on weekends, adjust accordingly.

Step 9: Select Keywords

Keywords are the backbone of your Google Ads campaign. Use precise and relevant keywords to attract high-quality leads. Avoid broad-match keywords, which can trigger ads for irrelevant searches. Instead, use phrase match and exact match types to ensure your ads appear only for searches that are highly relevant to your services. Email me at Cooper@wiseguysdm.com for a curated list of keywords that have proven effective for estate planning attorneys.

- **Broad Match:** This is the default setting and will show your ads for searches that Google deems relevant, even if they don't contain your keywords. This can result in wasted ad spend on irrelevant searches. For example, using a broad match for "estate planning lawyer" might trigger ads for unrelated queries like "how to become a lawyer."
- **Phrase Match:** This option shows your ads only when the search query contains your keyword phrase in the exact order but with words before or after. For example, using phrase match for "estate planning lawyer" could trigger ads for searches like best "estate planning lawyer" near me. This is the match type we use 99% of the time.
- **Exact Match:** This option gives you total control, showing your ads only for searches

that match your keyword exactly or very closely. For example, using exact match for [estate planning lawyer] will only show your ad for searches that precisely match this term or a close variant, ensuring maximum relevance.

Step 10: Create Compelling Ads

Write ads that speak directly to your target audience's needs. Highlight the benefits of choosing your firm and include a clear call to action. For example, an ad might read, "Need an Estate Planning Lawyer? Protect Your Family's Future. Call Now for a Free Consultation!" Use ad extensions to provide additional information, such as your phone number, links to specific service pages, and business location. These extensions can increase your ad's visibility and make it easier for users to take action.

Step 11: Develop a High-Quality Landing Page

Your landing page should be directly related to the ad's message and provide a seamless user experience. Include clear information about your services, client testimonials, and a strong call to action. Ensure the page is mobile-friendly and loads quickly to avoid frustrating users. A good landing page should include the following:

- **Relevant Content:** The content on your landing page should match the ad that led visitors there. For example, if your ad promises estate planning services, the landing page should provide detailed information about those services.
- **Clear Call to Action (CTA):** Include a prominent CTA, such as "Schedule a Free Consultation," to guide users toward taking the next step.
- **Trust Signals:** Use client testimonials, industry certifications, and privacy assurances to build trust with potential clients. Including client logos, professional affiliations, and awards can also enhance credibility.
- **Easy Navigation:** Make it simple for users to find the information they need and to contact your firm. Present information using clear headings, bullet points, and concise paragraphs.

Step 12: Set Up Conversion Tracking

Implement tracking codes to measure the effectiveness of your campaign. This data will help you understand which ads and keywords are driving leads and allow you to optimize accordingly. Use

Google's conversion tracking features to set up goals for phone calls, form submissions, and other valuable actions. This information will provide insights into which aspects of your campaign are most effective and where adjustments may be needed.

MAXIMIZING YOUR CAMPAIGN'S EFFECTIVENESS

To ensure your Google Ads campaign consistently generates quality leads, adhere to these golden rules:

- **Focus:** Each service you want to promote should have its own campaign with specific keywords, ads, and landing pages. This targeted approach improves relevance and conversion rates. For example, create separate campaigns for wills, trusts, and power of attorney services, each tailored to attract clients looking for those specific services.
- **Track Results:** Use tracking numbers and Google's conversion tracking to monitor your campaign's performance. Understand which ads are driving the most leads and adjust your strategy accordingly. Regular analysis

helps identify successful tactics and areas that need improvement.
- **Consistency:** Regularly check your ads, update your negative keyword list, and make adjustments based on performance data. Consistent monitoring and optimization will improve results over time. Schedule routine reviews of your campaign to adjust bids, pause underperforming ads, and experiment with new keywords.
- **Patience:** Successful Google Ads campaigns don't yield results overnight. Allow your campaigns to run for at least a few weeks before making drastic changes, giving Google's algorithms time to optimize.

THE IMPORTANCE OF AN AMAZING LEAD INTAKE PROCESS

Even the best Google Ads campaign will fall short if you don't have an effective lead intake process in place to handle incoming inquiries. A well-structured lead intake process is crucial for converting leads into clients and maximizing the return on your ad spend. This process begins the moment a potential client contacts your firm, whether through a phone call, email, or web form submission. How you handle this initial contact can make or break your chances of turning a lead into a loyal client.

1. **Prompt Response:** Responding to inquiries quickly is critical. Studies show that the faster you respond, the more likely you are to convert a lead. Implement a system that allows your team to respond to leads within minutes. Consider using automated responses that acknowledge receipt of the inquiry and provide the next steps, but always follow up with a personal touch as soon as possible.
2. **Train Your Staff:** Ensure that your team is trained to handle inquiries professionally and efficiently. They should know how to ask the right questions to understand the lead's needs and how to communicate the value of your services. Role-playing different scenarios can help staff feel prepared and confident in managing conversations with potential clients.
3. **Qualify Leads:** Not every lead will be a perfect fit for your firm. Develop a script or checklist to qualify leads quickly and effectively. Identify key indicators of a high-quality lead, such as the type of service

needed, urgency, and willingness to schedule a consultation. This helps you focus your efforts on the most promising prospects.
4. **Follow-Up:** Many leads won't convert on the first contact. Have a structured follow-up system in place to keep your firm top of mind. Use a CRM system to track interactions and set reminders for follow-up calls or emails. Providing additional resources, such as a free e-book or informational guide, can help nurture leads who aren't ready to commit immediately.
5. **Personalization:** Tailor your follow-up communication based on the information gathered during initial contact. Personalized emails or phone calls that reference specific details discussed can create a stronger connection and demonstrate that your firm understands and cares about the lead's unique situation.

THE POWER OF GOOGLE ADS IN ESTATE PLANNING MARKETING

Google Ads, when executed correctly, can become a highly efficient tool for generating leads and growing your estate planning law firm. By focusing on relevance, quality, and continuous optimization, you can leverage Google's vast reach to connect with prospects actively searching for your services.

However, the success of your Google Ads efforts doesn't stop at generating leads; it also depends on having an effective lead intake process to ensure those leads are nurtured and converted into clients. Follow the steps outlined in this chapter, and invest in building a strong lead intake system, and you'll be well on your way to a successful Google Ads strategy that drives meaningful business results.

CHAPTER 5
GENERATING BUSINESS WITH WEBINARS

Once your local SEO and Google Ads campaigns are up and running, you can expand to generate leads and new clients through webinars.

In chapter two, I touched on this briefly when I spoke about being seen as the expert and using webinars to generate content.

In this chapter, I will break down how you can use webinars to establish your authority and attract new clients to your estate planning law firm.

To succeed with webinars, focus on three main components:

1. Create a Great Webinar
2. Market The Webinar
3. Follow Up

CREATE A GREAT WEBINAR

The first step is creating a webinar your target audience will want to attend. Without this, the rest of the steps in this chapter will be a huge waste of time. To ensure your webinar attracts the right audience, you need to clearly identify who you want to reach.

Are your clients primarily retirees concerned about passing on their legacy? Or are they young families just beginning to think about their financial future? Knowing who you're speaking to allows you to tailor your content to their specific concerns, making your webinar informative and highly relevant.

For example, a generic webinar titled "Understanding Estate Planning" is too broad and will not catch the attention of anyone. You want your webinar to resonate with your target audience, prompting them to think, "This is exactly what I need!"

Let's look at a better approach. Suppose your target audience is business owners. A specific concern might be: "What happens to my business if I pass away unexpectedly?" With this focused topic, you're much closer to creating a successful webinar. Always remember, people buy with emotions and justify with logic. Estate planning is a deeply emotional area, and your target market must understand and utilize your services before it's too late.

TIPS FOR CRAFTING YOUR WEBINAR CONTENT

- **Focus on Real-Life Scenarios:** Share case studies or hypothetical situations that your audience can relate to. For instance, discuss how a lack of estate planning could lead to prolonged probate processes or family disputes. Personal stories create emotional connections and make the information more relatable.
- **Include Visual Aids:** Use slides, graphics, and charts to illustrate complex concepts. Visual aids can help make your content more engaging and easier to understand. For example, you could use a flowchart to show the steps involved in creating an estate plan

or a timeline graphic to explain how an estate plan evolves with life changes.

- **Interactive Elements:** Incorporate Q&A sessions, polls, or surveys to engage your audience. Interaction keeps attendees involved and provides valuable insights into their concerns and questions. For example, a poll question like "What's your biggest concern about estate planning?" can offer real-time feedback and make the audience feel heard.
- **Expert Guest Speakers:** Consider inviting guest speakers, such as financial advisors, tax professionals, or other estate planning attorneys, to provide additional perspectives. This can enhance the value of your webinar and attract a wider audience.
- **Educational and Actionable Content:** Educate your audience about estate planning basics, but also give them actionable steps they can take. For instance, outline a three-step process to start their estate planning journey or a checklist to ensure their current estate plan is up to date. This helps establish you as a knowledgeable resource and increases the likelihood of attendees seeking your services.

RESOURCES FOR CREATING ENGAGING WEBINARS

While I specialize in the marketing side, several resources can help you master the art of creating compelling webinar content. I recommend:

- **Expert Secrets by Russell Brunson:** This book provides insights on how to position yourself as an expert in your field, crafting your message and delivering it effectively. It's a great resource for understanding the psychology behind why people attend webinars and how to engage them.
- **One Too Many by Jason Fladlien:** This book dives into creating webinars that convert, focusing on structuring your presentation to lead attendees from interest to action. It covers everything from scripting your webinar to handling objections and closing sales.

MARKETING YOUR WEBINAR

Once your webinar is ready, it's time to market it effectively. Without a targeted marketing strategy, your efforts may fall flat. Here's how to get started:

CHOOSE THE DATE OF YOUR WEBINAR

Timing is critical. I've found that Thursday or Friday afternoons tend to work best for attendance. This is when people are more likely to be available and attentive. Avoid early mornings or late afternoons to ensure better participation. Plan to promote your webinar for at least two weeks to build excitement and anticipation. This window allows you to reach your audience multiple times and increase registration numbers.

CREATE YOUR LANDING PAGE

Your landing page is the gateway to your webinar. It serves as a registration page where attendees sign up. Keep the design simple and focused:

- **Headline:** Make the headline the exact topic of your webinar. For example, "What Happens to Your Business If You Pass Away Unexpectedly? Essential Estate Planning for Business Owners." This immediately communicates the benefit of attending the webinar.
- **Key Takeaways:** Highlight three to four main points attendees will learn. Focus on the

benefits and outcomes they can expect. For example, "Learn how to protect your business, avoid family disputes, and ensure a smooth transition of ownership."

- **Social Proof:** Include testimonials, past success stories, or any recognition your firm has received. Social proof can significantly increase trust and credibility. Consider adding logos of reputable organizations you've worked with or client testimonials that speak to your expertise.
- **Visual Appeal:** Use professional images, clean layouts, and branding elements consistent with your firm's identity. A visually appealing landing page can enhance credibility and engagement.
- **Clear Call-to-Action:** Ensure the registration process is straightforward. Collect names and email addresses, explaining how attendees will receive their webinar link. Offering something valuable, like a checklist or e-book, upon registration can also incentivize sign-ups. For example, "Register now and receive our free checklist: '5 Essential Steps for Business Owners in Estate Planning.'"

Feel free to email me at Cooper@wiseguysdm.com if you need templates for high-performing registration pages. Having a solid example can streamline your process.

CREATE YOUR EMAIL FOLLOW-UP AND REMINDERS

Automated email follow-ups are essential. Upon registration, attendees should receive an immediate confirmation email with all necessary details. Sending daily reminders leading up to the webinar keeps the event top of mind, and sharing tidbits of what they'll learn helps maintain excitement.

- **Confirmation Email:** This should include the date, time, and link to the webinar. Reiterate the value of the webinar and what they will gain by attending.
- **Reminder Emails:** Send reminders one week before, the day before, and the morning of the webinar. These emails should include compelling reasons to attend, such as key points of the presentation or special offers available only to attendees.

Expert Tip: Include a calendar link for scheduling a consultation in the confirmation and reminder emails. This simple addition can lead to immediate client inquiries. Even if they can't attend the webinar, they might still want to consult with you.

CREATING THE MARKETING CAMPAIGN

With your content, landing page, and email sequences ready, it's time to launch your marketing campaign. Here's how to proceed:

Utilize Your Current Database

Start by reaching out to your existing database of clients and leads. These individuals are already familiar with your firm, making them more likely to engage.

- **Segment Your Email List:** Send personalized invitations to different segments of your list based on their interests and past interactions. For example, previous clients might receive a different invitation than new leads or partners.
- **Highlight Exclusive Benefits:** Make your email recipients feel special by offering

exclusive insights or early access to the webinar content.

Social Media Ads

Creating effective social media ads is crucial. Think of social media ads as a way to capture attention in a crowded space. Make your ads resonate with your target audience's specific needs and desires.

- **Ad Copy:** Write compelling, benefit-driven copy. Highlight why your webinar is a must-attend event. For example, "Learn how to secure your business's future—register for our free webinar on essential estate planning for business owners."
- **Visuals:** Use eye-catching visuals that align with your brand. Consider using professional graphics that relate to your topic. Images of families, businesses, or professional settings can create a visual connection with the content.
- **Video Ads:** Consider creating a short video ad where you invite your target audience to the webinar. This adds a personal touch and can increase trust and credibility.
- **Audience Targeting:** Utilize precise targeting options available on platforms like Facebook

and Instagram. Target demographics, interests, and behaviors relevant to your ideal client base. For example, target business owners within a specific age range or those who have shown interest in financial planning.
- **A/B Testing:** Create different versions of your ads and test them to see which performs better. Change elements like headlines, images, and calls to action to identify what resonates most with your audience.

Explore Joint Ventures

Partnering with complementary businesses can expand your reach. Look for companies that serve the same market but aren't direct competitors. In exchange for mutual benefits, they could help promote your webinar through their channels.

- **Find the Right Partners:** Look for financial advisors, accountants, or real estate agents who deal with clients needing estate planning services. Approach them with a proposal that outlines mutual benefits.
- **Promotional Exchange:** Offer to promote their services to your audience in exchange for them promoting your webinar to their

clients. This can include email marketing, social media posts, or mentions in newsletters.
- **Co-Host Webinars:** Consider co-hosting a webinar with a partner. This can bring a broader audience and provide added value by combining expertise. For example, a webinar with both a lawyer and a financial advisor can offer a comprehensive view of estate planning.
- **Incentivize Participation:** Offer exclusive deals or bonuses to clients referred by your joint venture partners, increasing the incentive for both partners to participate actively.

THE FOLLOW-UP SEQUENCE

The real value often comes after the webinar. Even with excellent attendance rates, only a fraction of registrants might attend the live webinar. A strong follow-up strategy is crucial:

Send a Webinar Replay

Immediately after the webinar, send a recording to all registrants. Emphasize the importance of the content and provide a direct link to view the replay. Consider creating a dedicated page on your website for this replay, highlighting key points and offering additional resources.

- **Email Subject Line:** Use a compelling subject line to increase open rates. For example, "Missed Our Webinar on [topic]? Watch the Replay Now!"
- **Personalized Follow-Up:** Personalize the follow-up emails by addressing attendees by name and mentioning specific points discussed during the webinar. This can increase engagement and make them feel valued.

Repurpose the Webinar Content

Maximize the value of your webinar by repurposing the content:

- **YouTube Upload:** Upload the full recording to your firm's YouTube channel. Optimize the title and description with keywords related to estate planning to improve searchability.
- **Social Media Clips:** Create short clips from the webinar to share on social media. Highlight key points or particularly engaging

moments. Use captions for better accessibility and engagement.
- **Blog Post:** Write a blog post summarizing the webinar's main points. Include a call to action encouraging readers to watch the full recording or contact your firm for more information.
- **Podcast Episode:** If you have a podcast, use the webinar audio as an episode. Alternatively, launch a podcast series featuring your webinars to reach an even broader audience.
- **Downloadable Resources:** Based on the webinar content, create additional resources, such as a downloadable eBook or checklist. Use these as lead magnets to capture contact information on your website.

RINSE AND REPEAT

Conducting webinars regularly—such as quarterly—allows you to continually build your email list and engage with potential clients. Over time, you'll gain insights into what works best for your audience, refining your approach for even better results. This consistency helps establish your firm as a trusted authority in estate planning. Your firm will start to generate referrals and repeat business on a consistent basis.

- **Analyze and Optimize:** After each webinar, analyze attendance, engagement, and feedback. Use this data to improve future webinars. Identify which topics and marketing strategies yield the highest engagement and conversions.
- **Build a Webinar Library:** Create a library of past webinars on your website. This will serve as a valuable resource for potential clients and demonstrate your firm's expertise and commitment to education.

WRAPPING IT UP

Implementing a webinar strategy requires dedication, planning, and consistent effort. However, once you have a process in place, it becomes a powerful tool for generating steady leads and growing your estate planning law firm. With each webinar, your reach expands, your list of contacts grows, and your position as an industry expert solidifies.

CHAPTER 6
HOW TO GENERATE REFERRALS FROM YOUR TARGET MARKET

It is no secret that referrals are the best leads and clientele your law firm will receive. Creating rock-solid referral partners is one of the best things you can do for your law firm. The question is, what is the best way to do this?

I stole this tactic from Chet Holmes in his book The Ultimate Sales Machine. I use it for my company and all of my estate planning clients, and it works wonders! Here is the strategy in a nutshell: "The Dream 100 is based on the idea that it's more effective to focus sales efforts on a smaller number of dream clients than trying to reach a larger number of prospective customers."

Remember what I said in the first chapter about the power of focus? This strategy expands on this. But instead of trying to make sales to your customers, we are going to focus on generating referral partners. Here is a short list of dream referral partners you should be targeting.

- Financial Advisors and Planners
- Accountants and CPAs
- Family Law Attorneys
- Wealth Managers
- Personal Injury Attorneys
- Bank Trust Officers

Imagine if 10 to 20 of these people referred clients to your law firm on a daily basis. That would make a massive difference in your law firm's bottom line. I have clients who have implemented this strategy and receive 30-40 quality referrals a month from just a handful of referral partners.

The main goal of your marketing efforts is to not have to rely on one single lead generation source. So, if the leads generated from Local SEO are slow for one month, you can rest easy knowing that you have referrals and Google Ads working for you as well. It is very rare that all of these avenues are slow together. It just doesn't happen.

There is no better feeling in the world than knowing with absolute certainty that your law firm will always have hot leads banging down your door. Almost every problem in your business can be solved with new sales. Let's break down the Dream 100 strategy for your law firm.

Quick note: While I was writing this, I sent a rough draft to a handful of clients. They came back to me and said they loved the chapter but asked, "Couldn't you use this strategy for your dream clients as well?"

Of course, you can. But first, get a handful of referral partners who refer you to a bunch of cases rather than going after a one-and-done situation. Focus on generating amazing referral partners, then move on to marketing to the consumer.

CREATING YOUR DREAM 100 STRATEGY

Let's discuss how to create your dream 100 strategy, which will produce results for your estate planning law firm.

- Gather Your List
- Choose Your Gifts
- Create Your Dream 100 Letters
- Create a Dream 100 Social Media Plan

- Create Your Dream 100 Calendar
- Conduct Dream 100 Follow-up Calls
- Create The Meeting

GATHER YOUR LIST

The first step is to choose which group from the list above you will focus on. Open an Excel spreadsheet and add all the contacts that you think would benefit your law firm the most. This step is all about quality over quantity. Also, it doesn't have to be exactly 100 prospects. Just ensure you add enough to make this strategy worthwhile.

When I create a Dream 100 list for my company, I personally go through and create it myself. It might take me a week or so, but it is very important to ensure you get your ideal prospects.

BAIT THE HOOK

Before you send anything to your Dream 100 list, you need to create something of value that will make them want to reach out to you.

The gifts and touches that we are sending out are like baiting the hook when you go fishing. If you drop down a hook without any bait on it or bait that the fish doesn't like to eat, the fish will not bite the hook, no matter how many times you drop it in front of its face. (Assuming the fish is all there mentally.) If you want to catch the fish, add something that it will want to bite! The same holds true for this process.

Create a presentation or a booklet that outlines a topic your Dream 100 referrals would truly want to learn about. Things that will allow them to make more money and be seen as the expert in their field by their customers. The more money you can help others make, the more money you will make. Every market and state is different, so ensure you create an offer that will resonate with your dream referral partner. If you reach out to me at Cooper@wiseguysdigitalmarketing.com, I can send you the best-performing examples from past clients.

CHOOSE THE GIFTS

The best way to get noticed by your dream referral partners is to send them small gifts every month. Choose cheap but useful gifts so it doesn't feel like you are trying to bribe them. Useful tools such as a penlight or a tape measure are held onto.

Here are a couple of examples of things we have sent in the past.

- Keychain flashlight
- Rubix Cube
- Flashlight pen
- Calculator
- Miniature tool kit

The best part about these gifts is that you can buy around one hundred of them for relatively cheap. I know I sound like a broken record, but if you reach out to me at Cooper@wiseguysdigitalmarketing.com, I will send you the list and where to purchase these items for cheap.

CREATE THE LETTERS

Please remember to include a brief, compelling letter with every gift you send. The letter should be concise and include an irresistible offer that the recipient can easily accept. It should also prompt them to take a specific action. Your offer will play a crucial role in the success of this strategy.

When targeting other businesses, your primary objective is to secure an appointment to present your information or proposal. Also, keep in mind that this approach involves a series of letters, not just one. The goal is to stand out and build brand awareness with potential referral partners. Remember, the letter should cleverly tie in with the gift you've sent. Think of it as a step towards the ultimate goal, much like softening up the prospect before making a direct pitch.

CREATE YOUR SOCIAL MEDIA PLAN

Most, if not all, of your Dream 100 referral partners will be on social media. Since this is going to be a business-to-business strategy, I recommend you focus your efforts on connecting with them on LinkedIn. Add them as a connection, and comment and like the things they share on their profiles.

The goal of this strategy is to be omnipresent in their world. But you can go over the top with these efforts, so ensure you are not creeping them out.

CREATE YOUR DREAM 100 CALENDAR

Once you have created your Dream 100 list, understand what you're going to send them, and have an offer that will make them want to reach out to you and learn more, you need to ensure you create your Dream 100 calendar.

Schedule the day you will send your packages and ensure they go out consistently on that day. If you don't put it on your calendar, it won't get done. If you send two or three gifts and then radio silence, that will do no good for your law firm.

CONDUCT YOUR DREAM 100 FOLLOW UP

The goal of all of the previous marketing efforts is to get your dream referral to notice your law firm. To do this, you will need to hire an assistant or a freelancer on Upwork.com to call and follow up with the packages and information you've been sending over and try to get them to agree to let you give your presentation. Give them a script, and ensure they follow it to a tee.

The main goal of this call is to get your dream referral on your calendars so you can present the information that you've been offering in the packages and letters you've been sending. I've learned that the most effective way to turn this list of dream referrals into actual referral partners is to conduct the presentation either in person or over Zoom. But the key is to ensure that you are offering something that benefits or adds value to the life of your dream referral partner. If you already have a handful of referral partners, ask them what they would like to see or what would catch their attention.

PRESENT OR SHARE YOUR INFORMATION

Once you have scheduled an appointment with your dream referral, you need to ensure that you follow through on the promises you made. Give them great information and show them how you can help them and their clientele succeed. When you do this correctly, you'll stand apart from all of your competitors vying for their attention.

YEAH, BUT...

Something I hear a lot is, "Almost all of these people already have an estate planning law firm they are close with."

Here's something that I've seen hundreds of times. As you continually follow up and establish yourself in your referral prospect's mind, as soon as their current provider or a partner lets them down in any way, who do you think they're going to turn to? The company that is persistently reaching out and vying for business. They're going to give you a chance because you've never given up and have established yourself as an authority in your market.

WRAPPING IT UP

When implemented correctly, the Dream 100 strategy will generate the best referral partners and grow your law firm faster than ever before. But I will say this is not an overnight thing. This takes time, determination, and persistence. you want your dream referrals to go from "I have no idea who this law firm is" to "I've heard of this law firm" to "Yes, I work with this law firm actively." This does not happen overnight, but it will with persistence and dedication.

Implement the tools and tactics in this chapter to create referral partners that grow your law firm like never before.

CHAPTER 7
PUTTING IT ALL TOGETHER

CHAPTER 2

Target Market: Defining your target market is the first step in any effective marketing strategy. Ask yourself who your ideal clients are—retirees, young families, business owners, or high-net-worth individuals—and tailor your marketing messages and services to meet their specific needs. Develop detailed client personas that include demographic information, goals, and pain points.

- **Branding:** Your brand should clearly communicate who you are and what you do. Choose a descriptive name for your firm that includes relevant keywords (e.g., "Estate Planning" or "Trusts and Estates"). Select colors that evoke trust and professionalism, such as blues and greens, and ensure your logo and other visual elements consistently reflect your brand identity. Document these elements in a brand guide to maintain consistency across all marketing channels.

- **Website:** A well-designed, mobile-first website is crucial for converting visitors into clients. Ensure your site loads quickly, is easy to navigate, and includes clear calls to action. Use professional images, compelling copy, and engaging video content to capture attention and build trust. Key pages should include a strong homepage, service descriptions, attorney bios, client testimonials, and a contact form. Regularly update your website with fresh content, such as blog posts or FAQs, to improve SEO and keep visitors engaged.
- **Expert Status:** Position yourself as an authority in estate planning by creating high-quality content that addresses common client concerns. Writing a book or whitepaper, hosting webinars, and publishing blog posts on relevant topics can showcase your expertise. Share this content on your website,

social media, and during consultations to build credibility and trust.
- **Social Media:** Use platforms like Facebook, LinkedIn, and Instagram to connect with your target audience. Share educational content, firm updates, and community involvement to engage followers. Use video content to increase engagement and humanize your firm. Run paid social media campaigns to boost visibility and attract new leads. Respond to comments and messages promptly to foster relationships.
- **Tracking:** Implement tracking tools like Google Analytics, CallRail, and CRM systems to monitor the effectiveness of your marketing efforts. Track website traffic, call volumes, lead sources, and conversions. Regularly review this data to understand which strategies are working and make adjustments as needed.

CHAPTER 3: LOCAL SEO – GETTING YOUR FIRM TO THE TOP OF LOCAL SEARCH

- **Importance of Local SEO:** Local SEO is essential for estate planning firms that want to attract clients in their geographic area. Appearing in the Local Map Pack (the top three local search results) can significantly increase visibility and drive more qualified leads to your firm.
- **Google Business Profile Optimization:** Claim and fully optimize your Google Business Profile. Include accurate NAP (Name, Address, Phone number) information, select relevant categories (e.g., Estate Planning Attorney), add high-quality photos, and regularly update your profile with posts about your services or firm news.
- **Consistency in NAP Information:** Ensure that your firm's name, address, and phone number are consistent across all online listings, including your website, directories, and social media profiles. Inconsistent NAP information can confuse search engines and hurt your local search rankings.

- **Building Local Citations:** Create and maintain listings on local business directories, legal directories, and review sites. These citations help improve your local SEO by reinforcing your firm's presence in the community. Focus on directories that are relevant to your practice area and location.
- **Gathering Client Reviews:** Encourage satisfied clients to leave positive reviews on your Google Business Profile and other review platforms. Reviews not only build trust with potential clients but also influence local search rankings. Develop a system for requesting reviews after a successful case or consultation, and respond to all reviews—positive and negative—to show that you value client feedback.
- **Website Optimization:** Create location-specific pages on your website that target the cities or regions you serve. These pages should include relevant keywords, local information, and calls to action. To further enhance your local relevance, regularly publish blog posts that address local estate planning issues or news.
- **Competitor Research:** Analyze the top-ranking law firms in your area to see what

they are doing right. Look at their website structure, content, keywords, and reviews. Identify gaps in their strategy that you can capitalize on, such as offering more in-depth content or targeting underserved locations.

CHAPTER 4: GOOGLE PAY-PER-CLICK ADS

- **Immediate Lead Generation:** Google Ads allow you to place your firm at the top of search results instantly, making them ideal for generating immediate leads. Focus on high-intent keywords that reflect your target clients' search behavior, such as "estate planning attorney near me" or "wills and trusts lawyer."
- **Understanding Quality Score:** Quality Score affects your ad placement and cost per click. Improve your Quality Score by optimizing the following:
- **Click-Through Rate (CTR):** Write compelling ad copy with strong calls to action to encourage clicks.
- **Keyword Relevance:** Ensure your ads closely match the keywords you're bidding on. Use

exact match and phrase match keywords to maintain relevance.
- **Landing Page Quality:** Direct users to landing pages that provide valuable information and are closely related to the ad content. Ensure the landing page loads quickly and offers a clear call to action.
- **Campaign Setup:** Follow these steps to set up your Google Ads campaign:
- **Define Campaign Objectives:** Set clear goals, such as generating phone calls, form submissions, or website visits.
- **Keyword Research:** Use tools like Google Keyword Planner to find relevant keywords. Focus on specific, high-intent keywords that reflect the needs of your target market.
- **Ad Copy:** Write concise, persuasive ads that highlight your firm's expertise and benefits. Include your target keywords in the headline and description.
- **Budget and Bidding:** Set a budget that aligns with your goals and choose a bidding strategy, such as cost per conversion or maximize clicks.
- **Ad Extensions:** Use ad extensions like call buttons, location information, and additional

links to provide more information and make it easier for users to contact you.
- **Negative Keywords:** Regularly update your list of negative keywords to exclude irrelevant searches and avoid wasting ad spend. Monitor search terms reports to identify keywords that are not generating quality leads.

CHAPTER 5: GENERATING BUSINESS WITH WEBINARS

- **Webinar Benefits:** Webinars are an excellent tool for showcasing your expertise, engaging with potential clients, and building trust. They allow you to provide valuable information while demonstrating your knowledge in a live, interactive format.
- **Creating a Great Webinar:** Choose a specific topic that addresses a common client concern or question, such as "The Top 5 Estate Planning Mistakes to Avoid." Plan your content to be informative and actionable, and practice delivering it confidently. Use a professional setup with good lighting and sound to enhance the quality of your presentation.

- **Marketing Your Webinar:** Promote your webinar through multiple channels:
- **Email Marketing:** Send invitations to your email list with details about the webinar topic and how to register.
- **Social Media:** Create event posts on platforms like Facebook and LinkedIn. Use paid ads to reach a broader audience.
- **Website:** Add a registration form on your website's homepage or a dedicated landing page.
- **Follow-Up:** After the webinar, follow up with attendees by sending a thank-you email, a link to the webinar recording, and additional resources related to the topic. Use the opportunity to schedule consultations or offer a special promotion.
- **Content Repurposing:** Use the recorded webinar to create various types of content:
- **Upload the full video to YouTube and your website.**
- **Edit short clips for social media posts.**
- **Transcribe the webinar into a blog post.**
- **Use the audio for a podcast episode.**
- **Create an e-book or guide based on the webinar content.**

CHAPTER 6: HOW TO GENERATE REFERRALS FROM YOUR TARGET MARKET

- **Dream 100 Strategy:** Identify your top 100 potential referral sources, such as financial advisors, accountants, real estate agents, and other professionals who interact with your target market. Build a list of these contacts and develop a plan to connect with them regularly.
- **Building Relationships:** Cultivate relationships with your Dream 100 through consistent, meaningful outreach. Send personalized emails, invite them to lunch or networking events, and share valuable content that can help them in their own businesses. Focus on providing value before asking for referrals.
- **Leveraging Success Stories:** Share case studies and client testimonials with your referral network to demonstrate the positive outcomes you achieve. Highlight specific examples that align with the services or interests of your referral sources' clients.
- **Joint Marketing Efforts:** Collaborate with referral sources on joint marketing initiatives,

such as co-hosted webinars, seminars, or educational workshops. This not only provides value to both of your client bases but also strengthens your relationship with referral partners.

STAYING TOP OF MIND

One last thing. Frequently I find that my estate planning clients—not all of them, but most—don't have any kind of strategy to stay top of mind with clients who have hired them in the past. Ensure you have an email marketing strategy created for past clients. You never know when they will need your services again.

WRAPPING IT UP

I hope the strategies and tactics outlined in this book help you take your estate planning law firm to the next level. The course included with this book will be an extremely valuable tool for implementing these strategies. It breaks down in greater detail what you need to do to generate leads and new customers for your law firm.

Of course, if you understand the importance of digital marketing for your law firm but simply don't have the time to implement these strategies, reach out to me, and we can discuss what it would be like to work together. Email me at Cooper@wiseguysdm.com, and we can set up a meeting to discuss this.

Thank you again!

Cooper Saunders

www.ingramcontent.com/pod-product-compliance
Lightning Source LLC
Chambersburg PA
CBHW031424210526
45464CB00005B/2039